D1740995

AND FINALLY...

Have you heard about the budgie who had to go on a diet? Or the surfing Santa? Did you know that scientists have designed an engine that can run on tangerine oil? Would you believe that there's a world record for sitting in spaghetti? Or for staying in a room full of snakes? And what about the pigs who go jogging?

Here for the first time in print are some of the funniest and most fascinating stories from *Newsround*: BBC children's television's regular news programme. *Newsround* has won the Harlequin Award for Children's Documentary TV programmes on two occasions.

And Finally . . .

Funny stories from
John Craven's Newsround

John Craven and Eric Rowan
Illustrated by Chris Winn

BBC/KNIGHT BOOKS

Copyright © British Broadcasting Corporation 1984
Illustrations copyright © British Broadcasting Corporation 1984

First published 1984 by the British Broadcasting Corporation/Knight Books

British Library C.I.P.

Craven, John, *1940–*
   And finally—.
   1. Animals—Anecdotes, facetiae, satire,
   etc.—Juvenile literature
   I. Title
   591   QL791

   ISBN 0-340-33320-0
        0-563-20195-9 (BBC)

Printed and bound in Great Britain for
Hodder and Stoughton Paperbacks, a
division of Hodder and Stoughton Ltd.,
Mill Road, Dunton Green, Sevenoaks,
Kent (Editorial Office: 47 Bedford
Square, London, WC1 3DP) by
Cox and Wyman Ltd.,
Cardiff Road, Reading.

Contents

Introduction

It's hard to believe that *Newsround* is now older than many of its viewers. The programme was born in April, 1972, and more than 2,000 editions later we are still reporting in our own special way from all over the world.

In fact I am writing this from the country of Bangladesh, during a break in filming for *Newsround Extra*. The plight of people less fortunate than ourselves has always been one of the programme's main concerns and in Bangladesh I'm reporting from a clinic where starving babies are brought back to full health again.

But although *Newsround* responds to such stories and to the big events that suddenly happen around the world the programme has its lighter side, which is reflected in this book. Right from the start, we decided to report good news as well as bad, and to look out for the off-beat, but still newsworthy happenings. And sometimes, we all remember *them* long after we've forgotten the more serious news.

Occasionally, such stories actually lead the programme, but usually they are the last item, following the words 'and finally'. So we thought it would be fun to look back over the years and gather some of our 'end stories' into this collection. We can't show you the original film or photos that went with them, so we are grateful to the illustrator Chris Winn who has filled in the visual side.

Leafing through the scripts brought back many happy memories for me. I know that many viewers look forward to our odd-ball stories, and love to shudder at the often awful pun. No matter how grim the rest of the news, after 'and finally' there's something happening in the world to make us smile. Thank goodness.

John Craven,
Dhaka, Bangladesh
Summer, 1984

Record Breakers

There seems to be no limit on crazy ways for crazy people to get their name in the record books. In 1981 an American DJ who wanted to promote the idea of Italian food decided to sink himself in spaghetti. He filled his bathtub with the slithery stuff and sat in it in order to establish the world spaghetti-sitting record – easily done, as no one had attempted anything so silly before.

$$*\qquad*\qquad*$$

Yet once a record is made, someone has to go further. A year later a student from Bristol sat in a bath of spaghetti from lunchtime on Friday till the following Tuesday: a stodgy stint of seventy-three hours. He was raising money for charity when he slithered into the record books. And the American DJ's entry just pasta-way.

$$*\qquad*\qquad*$$

Another record was an attempt to make and toss the world's biggest pancake. Bucketfuls of batter were poured into a giant two-metre non-stick frying pan, and it took almost an hour to cook. Despite a complicated scaffolding arrangement to flip the pancake over, the first attempt was a resounding flop. The determined record breakers tried again; it was a case of second time lucky, avoiding a flipping crisis.

In Australia in our hot summer of 1983, one hundred and fifty skiers set out to build the biggest snowball in the world. It took them just under three hours to build the massive ball, using shovels and spades to pack the snow together. A huge amount was needed, and just a bit of help was laid on by a snow mobile. When finally ready, it measured five metres high and weighed about five tonnes. It was meant to last until Christmas – a strange present for an Australian Santa.

*　　*　　*

Another biggest-ever attempt was the one to make a sandwich three metres tall. It happened in Baltimore USA as a joint operation between students and a local ice-cream parlour. It started at ground level, and layers of ham and cheese were piled on top. The super sarnie used up four and a half thousand slices of cheese and three thousand slices of ham before a halt was called. The huge pile was in danger of tipping over long before it reached three metres. It finished at one and a quarter metres: get your teeth around that!

Animal Enterprises

Everyone knows that New York is a violent city, but it's not just the people who make it so. A rabbit called Harvey looked innocent enough, but he bit at least sixteen people and had to be locked away from human company. What could be done with this belligerent bunny? Well, a charity organisation hired him to guard their offices. He roamed loose at night inside the building, and a notice was posted to warn intruders about Harvey's vicious ways. So this 'Thugs Bunny' worked for his lettuces.

*　　*　　*

Across the other side of America from New York, in Hollywood, the makers of a science fiction film called 'Hiss' advertised for snakes to be the stars and all sorts of snakes and their owners queued up hoping for fame. In true Hollywood tradition, studio executives refused to make a quick decision. But those snakes who didn't get parts were all offered 'slide-on' roles.

*　　*　　*

Another new hopeful who didn't make it was Priska, a seven-year-old boxer dog. She was chosen by the local theatre company in Worcester for a part in their play, and delighted everyone in rehearsal. But on the first night she got stage fright, sat on her haunches in the wings and refused to budge. On the second night she did go on — but after ten seconds she bolted. Priska never got a third chance.

Antipodean Exploits

Strange things may be expected to happen on the opposite side of the world, and in Australia visitors to an island are being warned to avoid the colour green at all costs. The grasshoppers on Flinders island, off the southern tip of Australia are reported to have developed a crazed obsession with the colour. An official said green paint, green curtains, and even green knickers on a washing-line have all fallen victim to the grasshoppers' insatiable jaws, and that anyone wearing green clothing could suffer a very unpleasant experience. So in Flinders it's clearly green for danger.

* * *

Also in Australia, a row broke out over that cuddly little creature, the koala. One of the country's senior ministers suggested that Australia should stop using the koala as a national mascot. He complained that instead of being adorable little animals, 'they're flea-ridden, smelly and scratchy', and, in his words, 'when you pick one up, it piddles all over you'. He caused a storm, as newspapers, television, and other politicians leapt to the defence of the koala. Australia's national airline, which uses koalas in its advertisements, told *Newsround* the koalas were a very successful sales force and would carry on. Despite all the rumpus, the koalas are bearing up well.

* * *

And from Wellington, the capital of New Zealand, came news that all the country's police dogs were to be issued with boots. There were seventy Alsatian dogs in the New Zealand force at the time, and each got two pairs of rubber boots. They were to be worn when the dogs went into action at incidents like fights in public houses, when their paws could get cut by broken glass. And as it was an item from New Zealand, maybe they wear Wellington boots.

Down on the Farm

Farm animals are fine in their place, but if they start to wander they can be a nuisance. One MP wrote to the City of London Corporation suggesting that they make owners of cows daub them with luminous paint to prevent them being a danger to traffic at night. It's the cows and heifers in Epping Forest (which is owned by the City of London) that caused the problem. The cows have rights to graze and wander there by an ancient Act of Parliament. So perhaps it's the cars that should be fitted with cow bumpers. What heifer next!

*   .   *   *

Also in Wales police were called to investigate what was thought to be a robbery in a shop. The constable sent to check discovered it was no burglar, but a sheep which was hiding under a counter. Somewhat sheepishly, he arrested the animal. His name was P.C. Andrew *Lamb*.

*   *   *

And in Northumberland, seven-year-old Jane just couldn't believe her eyes when she looked into her bedroom. For there, flopped out on the bed, was a real-life baby bull. Apparently the bullock, called Bertie, had escaped from his field nearby. When Bertie got to Jane's house, he pushed open the back door, ambled through the kitchen, and then climbed the

stairs to Jane's bedroom. The police were called, but they couldn't get Bertie to budge. After all, he did weigh about three hundred and thirty kilos. Eventually, his owner managed to shove a reluctant Bertie back to his field.

*   *   *

In Gloucestershire, when a farmer went to check eighteen of his cows in a field, he thought they'd all become ill. They couldn't stand up, and their eyes were glazed. Then he smelt their breath – and discovered to his amazement that all the animals were drunk! They'd been eating sugar beet which had turned to alcohol in their stomachs. Now, he's changing their diet, to stop it happening again.

*   *   *

Perhaps those cows would like to be in Germany where a herd is munching its daily ration of fodder served up on trays! Instead of letting cows graze, a firm there thinks it's found a more efficient way. The new idea is to replace meadows and fields with special basin-shaped indoor growing trays. It takes just eight days to produce the grass from sowing the seed to serving it up in real style, and it's not affected by the weather. Apparently the cows really look forward to having their dinner served up on a plate.

*   *   *

Wandering sheep can cause problems too. In a small Welsh town they couldn't keep a flock of sheep out of a local housing estate. The sheep kept breaking out of nearby fields and wandered into the estate. At first cattle grids prevented them – as they stop animals throughout Britain. But these Welsh sheep worked out ways of crossing the tricky grids by tip-toeing over them! One council official said the older sheep were teaching their young ones how to do it. Baa-let lessons?

*   *   *

Amazing Animals

A troupe of circus elephants got a nasty shock when a runaway dog suddenly joined in their act. People in the audience scrambled out of the big top when the elephants began to panic. The dog, an English bull terrier called Bo, had dashed into the ring at Gillingham in Kent, barking and snapping. It sank its teeth into Dum-Dum, who was leading the five elephants. The trainer, Nicki King, leapt clear as Dum-Dum roared with pain. But Bo clung on to Dum-Dum's trunk, and then went for some of the other elephants – getting a few kicks in return. Dum-Dum and her troupe made a full recovery, and the circus owners say that nobody was in danger. But they warned Bo to keep clear of the circus in future. Remember, elephants never forget!

Goldfish were in the news one October. In Tokyo police were trying to track down thieves who turned fish-nappers. They raided a pond and carried off goldfish and carp worth a total of three million yen – that's four thousand three hundred pounds! The police say that one of the fish, a carp which was seventy-nine centimetres long, won a National Fish Contest one year, and alone was worth more than two thousand pounds. That haul was gold fish in more than just name.

*   *   *

Meanwhile in Italy Signorina Carmello Tisco was travelling by train from Rome to Cassino. With her, she took her two goldfish in a jam jar. To her amazement, the ticket collector demanded more than six thousand lire – that's about four pounds – for their fare. At first, she thought he was joking – the sum was four times the cost of her own fare! But the regulations say that six thousand lire is the smallest amount that can be charged on the trains for livestock weighing less than twenty-five kilos. The goldfish didn't even weigh twenty-five *grammes* – but the Signorina still had to pay.

*   *   *

The star witness in a court case in Israel was, of all things, a parrot. The judge wanted the parrot to sing for him. There was a dispute over ownership, and one of the men claiming to be the real owner said he'd taught the bird to sing a certain German nursery rhyme. The judge ruled that if it could sing that rhyme, it belonged to him. If it couldn't, it didn't. And what happened? The man lost, because the parrot couldn't be persuaded to open its beak. Not even to say 'pretty Polly'!

*   *   *

Pot Pourri

Thousands of motorists and bus passengers heading in to London for work one April day got a surprise when they looked up at a huge billboard on a roundabout. Especially one – for the message, in massive letters, was for him: *Happy Birthday Ian*! *I love you, Anne*. It was Anne's idea to give her husband a birthday greeting he could never forget.

*　　*　　*

Five bearded Welshmen wearing only animal skins set off one August day on an unusual trek to Stonehenge, the mysterious circle of stones in Southern England. They took along a huge two-tonne block of stone. Thousands of years ago it's believed their ancestors dragged similar lumps of granite from the Preseli mountains to Salisbury Plain. Exactly why isn't certain, but the 1980s journey was in aid of a hospital charity. This time though, the journey's slightly different. The Welshmen used a tractor and trailer, and crossed the River Severn by the suspension bridge.

*　　*　　*

Our Members of Parliament talk about some unusual things at times – like the colour of phone boxes. Sometime ago, a number of MPs complained that since British Telecom split from the rest of the Post Office, they've been planning to spend thousands of pounds re-painting all seventy-seven thousand phone boxes. But British Telecom said everyone was getting upset about nothing. A few boxes were painted yellow, but only as an experiment to test the paint and to see if people liked them. No decision has been made on a new colour . . . they've been trying out blue and green boxes as well as yellow ones. Obviously, they believe in suiting all political parties!

*   *   *

A survey shows that classroom desks and chairs are lower than they used to be, even though children are getting bigger. A surgeon from Denmark says this means many children are growing up with back pains. Now he's launched a campaign to make things more comfortable in the classroom. Obviously, it's a *growing* problem!

*   *   *

Animal Antics

Could rabbits' ears help solve the world's energy problems? A man called Bill Schultz from Oregon in the USA has discovered that rabbits – with a body temperature of more than forty degrees centigrade – give off heat through their ears – and he used ten of the animals to heat his greenhouse! He estimated that – allowing for feeding costs – the rabbit-power scheme saved him twenty pounds a day in fuel. What he didn't say is how the rabbits reacted to being used as heaters. When the hot weather comes, he could end up with ten hot, cross, bunnies!

When Paul Gleeson, a blind maths teacher from Long Island, New York, received his university degree, he didn't see why his guide dog, called 'Hal', shouldn't get one too. After all, he claimed, Hal had sat next to him in class for three years. Surprisingly, the university agreed. So Hal, a golden retriever, became the proud owner of a certificate which showed he attended all the lessons in the science course. A dog-ter of education!

* * *

Security men brought in three extra helpers to guard a display of priceless jewels. The helpers were deadly *snakes*, and they were on duty at the exhibition in Stockholm, the capital of Sweden. Among the stones being guarded by the snakes was an enormous blue sapphire, worth about a hundred thousand pounds. The organisers hoped the snakes would deter any . . . slippery customers.

* * *

'Whistle while you work' didn't do any good for the Swiss mynah bird whose cage was hung above the platform of a railway station. He was such an expert at imitating the guards' whistles that several drivers set off with their trains by mistake. To foil the bird, the guards had to use hand signals – but that's not as efficient, and eventually the mynah was sold. He'd found the wrong station in life.

A parrot called Jacob once became a key witness to a pet shop break in. It all happened in Copenhagen in Denmark. Forty-three parrots and budgies were stolen – except for Jacob. The police found *him*, safe and sound, in the street outside. So Jacob was taken off to the police station to see if he would talk. But all he did was keep repeating his name and where he lived. Jacob was no stool pigeon.

*   *   *

Tigger the Terror was a cat who thought he was a dog. He lay in wait for people delivering things to his home in a Devon village, and he attacked three postmen, the milkman, the paperman, and even a cameraman who came to take his picture. Then the Post Office asked his owner to try to keep Tigger indoors when the letters arrived. A warning notice told visitors what to expect – a cat with a temper like a tiger.

*   *   *

Two men who were robbing a village sub-post office were frightened away by a black cat called Lucky. Lucky was in the garden when the men walked into the shop at Abbots Morton, in Worcestershire. The Post Mistress refused to hand over the money. Then, in came Lucky, who leapt on to the back of one of the robbers, sinking her claws into him. He yelled, and both men ran off, empty-handed.

Unlikely Inventions

Remarkable invention stories reach us frequently: this one comes from Russia. It's a pair of boots with a big difference. Each boot contains a small petrol engine. And the motors transmit so much power to the soles of the feet that whoever wears them can stride along in giant three-metre steps – that's at least three times bigger than normal. But Russian pedestrians aren't likely to rush off for a pair – the boots weigh almost six kilos, and you have to carry a can of petrol to keep them going. So they're not even as effective as seven-league boots in old fairy tales.

*   *   *

For those people who long to see themselves as others see them, an unusual product went on sale in America. It was called a Rorrim – that's mirror spelt backwards. Unlike ordinary mirrors, the rorrim shows a true reflection and doesn't reverse the image. So when you comb your hair, your parting on the left-hand side, appears on the right in the rorrim. And what's more, when you turn the rorrim upside down, it shows *you* upside down. Very confusing – especially for *DNOURSWEN* snaf!

*   *   *

And from Finland comes news of an invention to please animal lovers. It's a painless mousetrap, and it took its inventor *thirty years* to work out. The trap looks like a box, and if a mouse touches the bait it will drop through a trapdoor, unharmed, into a cell below. The only trouble with this invention is that no one has suggested what you should *do* with the mouse once it was caught. Perhaps in another thirty years the inventor will provide the answer?

*   *   *

Panda-monium

In 1977 we had a story about Lan Lan, and her mate Kang Kang, adult pandas given to Tokyo zoo by the Chinese authorities. After five years in Tokyo, zoo vets were confidently expecting a happy event – the birth of the first baby panda in captivity outside China. Crowds gathered at the zoo, and Japan was swept by panda fever. Millions of panda toys flooded on to the market, from little cuddly creatures to giant-size working models selling for hundreds of pounds. Even the bakers prepared for the bonanza, making extra large biscuits in a panda shape. But Lan Lan had been having everyone on she had been getting fat just through eating too much.

* * *

Four years later, we showed pictures from China of Ching Ching, five, and Tau Tau, eight, having their annual medical check up. China, the only country where pandas live wild, has had more success breeding than anywhere else, and eleven pandas have been born in captivity. Vets there use machines just like the ones used on human beings to check the panda's heartbeats, while the patients chew their favourite food of bamboo shoots. Talk about pandered pandas!

* * *

Monstrous Tales

Monsters and dinosaurs keep turning up on *Newsround*! One monster who's supposed to live in Lake Champlain, in the American state of Vermont, has been nicknamed Champ. And although no one could prove he actually exists local people passed a law forbidding anyone to 'harm, harass or destroy' Champ. But before anyone could do that, they have to *find* the creature. Though many people have reported seeing the monster, no one has ever taken a picture. Sounds a bit like our own Nessie, up in Loch Ness. The first sighting reported this century (legends about a monster in Loch Ness go back hundreds of years) date from 1933. Since then, thousands of people have sought Nessie unsuccessfully. No photographs which prove her existence beyond doubt have ever been taken, and sophisticated underwater echo-location systems have failed to locate her. Nessie and Champ: a pair of very modest monsters.

*　　　*　　　*

Also, in America, scientists studying a set of dinosaur footprints have come up with some startling statistics which destroy the dinosaur's traditional image as a plodding, slow creature. By measuring the distance between dinosaur prints, they've calculated that some dinosaurs could move faster than the fastest humans. So if Sebastian Coe was in a race against this kind of dinosaur, he'd probably come second. Coe's top speed is eight metres a second. Dinosaurs could scamper nearly twelve metres a second.

*   *   *

And two rival teams of American explorers maintain that dinosaur-like animals may still be prowling the swamps of Africa. Local pygmies have described a creature that may be a survivor of a dinosaur species believed extinct for sixty million years. Now a biologist says he's discovered large footprints twenty-five centimetres wide and is convinced that large, unknown animals exist. The footprints were found in the Congo, near the Likuoala River, and could be from an animal related to the brontosaurus. More sightings were made by another team, at a nearby lake, where a creature with a smooth long neck and snake-like head was seen. Some photographs were taken but because it was dark, they did not come out. We'll just have to wait and see what develops!

*   *   *

Well Really!

Americans who dreamed of the wide-open spaces of the prairies have been given the chance to buy their own ranch at the incredibly cheap price of twelve pounds fifty pence! The snag was that the land was on the planet Mercury, one hundred and fifty-five million kilometres from earth. But Americans can buy a document, declaring them to be the owner of an enormous plot the size of London. It was the idea of a society for Astronomers that needed to raise money – and it did. All the customers saw was a photograph of Mercury taken by a space probe. That may have been just as well ... there's no air on Mercury, and the temperature is 426° centigrade. Hot property!

*   *   *

A story from Athens ended *Newsround* one evening. A soldier was told to guard four Mirages – jet fighter planes with long, tapering nosecones – that were on their way to the Middle East. But the sight of those long noses was too much for him. He hauled himself up on to one of them and started to swing backwards and for-wards by his hands. To his horror the nose slowly curved under his weight and he couldn't straighten it out again. So he decided the only answer was a quick swing on the other three planes so at least they'd all look the same shape. But soon someone noticed that all was not well with the multi-million pound planes, and technicians had to work for thirty-six hours to put the noses straight again.

They can sell anything in London auction rooms, even money. In a rare bank note sale one remarkable specimen was an Australian one pound note issued by the bank of Melbourne in 1857. It bore the nickname of 'Shinplaster', because the gold prospectors of those days used to keep money in their long socks for safety. The banks were wise to this so they covered the notes in flour. When the flour got mixed in with sweaty feet the notes tended to fall apart, so the banks could refuse to honour them. Hence they have a rarity value! The £1 note changed hands at £475!

*　　　*　　　*

From York one day came a story about a crazy carpet that caused some unusual problems. The carpet had a striking pattern of bright green, blue and yellow stripes, and it made some people who walked on it feel quite ill. They claimed that just looking at it made them dizzy and sick, and even lose their balance. And where was this potentially lethal floor covering? Why, in a brand new district hospital! So the victims of the crazy carpet didn't have to go far for treatment.

*　　　*　　　*

In Japan, one of the country's biggest makers of cars and motorbikes has been experimenting with a new kind of fuel. Scientists have designed an engine to run on oil that's been squeezed from *tangerines*. Only the peel is used, and the special oil has been tested successfully on a small car, and on two motorbikes. But there was one small snag. It took the peel of eleven thousand tangerines to make just one litre of oil. That would cost about four hundred and fifty pounds! With petrol in Japan costing about thirty-five pence, tangerine oil doesn't have a lot of a-peel!

*　　*　　*

Someone who passed through Heathrow in 1983 could well be the oldest man in the world. Sayeed Abdul Mahood, who comes from Pakistan, has a passport which gives his birth date as December 1823. His friends say it's true, but some officials think there may have been a mistake. Mr Mahood didn't say anything about his age, but airline officials reported that he looked amazingly well – not a day over a hundred and forty.

*　　*　　*

In 1981, the small Spanish town of Li-har decided to carry on, for the time being, its hundred-year-old war with France. The war broke out in the 1880s, but so far no one has been hurt and not a single shot has been fired. The mayor of that time decided to start the war because the French had insulted the Spanish King, Alfonso the Twelfth. He'd gone to Paris for an official visit, but the French government didn't look after him properly. To defend the King's honour, the mayor of Li-har declared war. For nearly a century nothing happened. Then, in 1976, King Juan Carlos of Spain made a trip to France. This time, all went well and the citizens of Li-har thought they'd make peace with France. But up to now, the French government still haven't signed the peace treaty. So, for the time being, the war that never was goes on. And a Spanish town with a population of less than a thousand people is officially at war with France.

*   *   *

Traffic jams in a city that doesn't have any roads? Yes, in Venice, which is famous for its network of canals. The problem comes from the thousands of boats that ply their way up and down the canals. The jams have become so bad that the boatmen of Venice, the gondoliers, demanded action. They also complained their passengers were getting bumpy rides because of the waves caused by speeding motorboats coming the other way. So signs saying 'SENSO UNICO' – that's Italian for 'one-way only' – went up along seventeen canals. They were added to a scheme which started several years ago. And now several kilometres of waterway are covered. The result is that people in small boats are getting a safer ride in the narrow alleyways – and the gondoliers are happy because holidaymakers can once again enjoy exploring the old city in comfort.

*   *   *

American Animal Escapades

Every day for a year, researchers at Arizona State University took some pigs for an early morning jog. It was part of an experiment to find out how regular jogging affects humans. Pigs were chosen for the project because their bodies work quite like ours. And – like people – pigs eat a lot of junk food. Some pigs took it easy at home while the others went jogging, and scientists compared their health. They proved that pigs who went jogging ate less than lazy ones, and, by the end of the research, they were much slimmer. There's no information about how the researchers got on.

*　　　*　　　*

Another animal story from America concerned a giraffe called Tennessee. He got stuck in the mud while strolling across a river in his safari park – and broke his leg. The vet was called in and after three hours' work managed to fix Tennessee's leg with a fibre-glass cast. It took about six weeks for the leg to set, but Tennessee just carried on taking his daily stroll in the longest cast ever.

*　　　*　　　*

Actually American vets do some incredible things, and one story with a happy ending was about a duck called Donna. Donna had been shot with an arrow, but carried on flying around as if nothing had happened. It took hours to trap Donna on a lake in Nevada. Every time the vets got close, she flew away, despite the dart through her breast. Finally though, they succeeded, and a helicopter rushed the injured Donna to an animal hospital to remove the deadly arrow. If only she'd ducked!

*   *   *

Bubbles was a runaway hippopotamus who escaped from her enclosure at a safari park in California. After she ambled to freedom, Bubbles spent most of her time under the water of a private pond some distance from the park . . . coming out only to feed. The park rangers managed to get her in the sights of their tranquilliser gun, but she got away again. For two-tonne truant, Bubbles, a narrow *squeak*!

*   *   *

Some years ago a very strange case caught the Chicago police on the hop. It was the case of the two-metre tall kangaroo, which was roaming round the skyscraper blocks of America's second city. Nobody knew where the kangaroo came from – it suddenly appeared, and the police weren't very good at arresting it. Two of them tried, and got a clout from the kangaroo before it bounded off.

The story hopped back into the headlines later when two kangaroos were spotted on the run near Milwaukee about one hundred and sixty kilometres away. Reports poured into the local Sheriff's office from startled Americans who just didn't expect to see a runaway 'roo. There was a false clue when a footprint turned out to belong to a deer. To add to the mystery, no one reported any kangaroos missing. The Sheriff was baffled, and according to reports reaching *Newsround*, the animals continued to be always one jump ahead.

Channel Crossings

Every summer one popular way to raise money for charity is to find a new daft way to cross the thirty-four kilometres of the English Channel. One, in 1977, was 'The Voyage of the Pink Loo'. With a bathroom suite of tub, basin and loo fixed to a motorised raft three soldiers floated across to France at a speed of about three knots. They reached the other side in ten hours, but when a storm blew up decided not to return the same way. Although *flushed* with success perhaps they were afraid they'd *loos* their way!

*　　　*　　　*

In August 1981 one twenty-year-old set out from Dover to paddle over in a bath tub. He wanted to prove British baths were best – but the French authorities were not at all happy about the strange craft because of the danger to shipping. He must've been in hot water when he landed!

*　　　*　　　*

One month later another strange crossing was made by a powered hang glider. Two Scotsmen clad in kilts – but cannily wearing wet suits underneath – made it to Calais in fifty minutes. It was the first ever crossing by hang glider. A piper at Dover played them off, so I suppose you could call it the latest Highland Fling!

Animal Professionals

Sparky was a black stray cat who was employed by the workers in a factory in Blackburn, Lancashire, to catch mice – unfortunately he had very bad luck. Sparky didn't catch a single mouse, and within a week of starting to patrol he broke his leg. He was given time off for an operation, but afterwards hobbled because of the pin in his leg. The workers clubbed together to pay the fees for Sparky's operation, and his meals came from petty cash. He was never given the sack, so I should think the mice were laughing!

*   *   *

Postmen collecting from letter boxes in Pembrokeshire in South Wales were amazed to find that some of the letters had bits missing. They discovered the boxes had been invaded by *snails*. And even when they were all cleared out, the snails came back again for a good nibble at the letters. The Post Office said that all *they* could do was to stick a note on the letters saying: 'Sorry, damaged by snails'.

*   *   *

A London pet shop owner used two furry monsters to guard his shop at night. When he locked up to go home, he let two tarantula spiders loose in his darkened shop, to frighten off intruders. He even had a warning notice in his shop window. 'Danger, these premises are patrolled by our tarantulas! They're cheaper to feed than guard dogs.' Each morning when he opened up, his first job was finding his guard spiders. But it was quite easy, or so he said. Tarantulas stay in a warm spot, and he caught them with a net.

*   *   *

Champion police dog Link had a secret of his own. At seven years old, he'd won the trials organised by the Avon and Somerset police. Afterwards, though, his handler was forced to admit that Link was missing some teeth. He'd had false fangs fitted, and the teeth had to be cemented in, so that he didn't leave them in the backside of any runaway criminal. So when Link was on duty, the teeth he bared were not all his own.

*   *   *

Reckless Wildlife

Thousands of minute bugs caused a giant problem at Bristol museum. A colony of mites infested many cases of stuffed animals, eating through all the fur and feathers of some exhibits. The mites also munched their way through a Maori cape worth fifteen thousand pounds! The museum had to be closed while fumigation experts summoned all their chemical might to stop the mites.

*   *   *

In Japan there was trouble from moths. It happened on a road bridge in the north of the country when a huge swarm of the insects formed a kind of carpet across the bridge. Startled motorists swerved and skidded out of control as they drove over the carpet, and police said at least nineteen cars crashed into each other. You could say the drivers were all of a flutter.

*   *   *

Also in Japan, a doctor who put an advertisement in the paper to try and find his missing dog got more than he bargained for. He didn't get his own dog back, but he did get others! They were all strays brought to him by people who saw his advert and felt sorry for him. He and his wife became fond of the new pets. So when angry neighbours complained about all the noise, they even decided to move house, rather than part with them. Their new home is in the mountains, well away from any other houses. It cost the doctor one hundred thousand pounds to build, but he says he can now give all his dogs a good home for the rest of their lives. But he doesn't want any more strays – he's got quite enough.

*   *   *

In Western Switzerland, when herds of wild boar damaged fields of wheat and maize, the local authorities thought up a rather unusual way of getting rid of the unwanted visitors. They didn't want to shoot the animals, just send them away from the cultivated area. So they drove them away with bad smells. A long row of rags dipped in a liquid repellent were staked out round the edges of the fields. It worked – the boars turned tail and ran all the way home.

*   *   *

A gang of nearly fifty vandals caused trouble in the monkey temple at Bristol Zoo. But for once the vandals weren't human – they were monkeys! The villains smashed most of the windows and caused a lot of damage. Another favourite trick was pulling concrete and plaster off the temple walls. The zoo officials had to instal armour-plated perspex in the windows. *Why* this colony of rhesus monkeys suddenly started to tear up its home was something of a mystery. It was normally a very happy group – there was very little gang warfare, and it could be that the monkeys were bored. Monkeys of course, are naturally quite destructive. But it wouldn't be surprising if the monkeys felt out in the cold – when they broke the windows they spoilt the temple's central heating system.

*　　*　　*

In Egypt monkeys started a riot in Cairo Zoo. Three which had unnaturally long hair had to be rescued by keepers after they were set upon by others in their enclosure. The three were given a haircut before they were put back and there was no more trouble.

Weather – like it or not

The weather always provides a fund of stories: there's certain to be somewhere in the world where the weather is not running true to form. One winter, we had a story about a dispute between two Italian ski resorts, when the villagers of Selva accused those in nearby Ortesi of stealing their snow. Tyre tracks led from the ski slopes of Selva to piles of snow, all ready to be spread on the bare hillsides of Ortesi. A local judge ruled that there was no law about stealing snow; but the people of Selva didn't want to lose their ski-ing surface. So they floodlit the ski slopes and hired armed guards to defeat the snow-rustlers!

And in Switzerland, where they're used to snow and have a reputation for a reliable railway system with trains which are always on time, that winter they weren't. Drivers on all the night-time trains in eastern Switzerland were ordered to cut their speed from the normal one hundred and twenty kilometres an hour to only thirty. The reason? To save the lives of wild animals, particularly deer. Because of the heavy snow-falls and cold the deer had left their homes in the forests and had taken to wandering closer to habitation, and often on to railway lines. In the daytime the drivers could slow down, but at night they couldn't spot the animals in time. So the trains were late, for once. You could say it was all due to hind-sight.

Icebergs made the *Newsround* headlines when a big conference was organised in the United States to discuss how the world might make use of them. Eighteen countries sent delegates and when they arrived — so did an iceberg! It was airlifted from the snows of Alaska five thousand kilometres to the conference centre in Iowa. True, it wasn't a very *big* iceberg, it weighed less than a tonne, but it was brought in as a symbol ... and as something to cool the delegates' drinks! It cost four thousand pounds to fly in the mini iceberg, and the bill was paid by a prince from Saudi Arabia. It must be the first time ever that ice has cost more than the drinks.

*   *   *

Snow in Miami, Florida, made the headlines too. Florida is the sunshine state, where rich Americans go in the winter to get away from the snow and the cold. But one year it did snow in Miami and even the turtles in the lagoon off the coast were in trouble. These are green sea turtles, but they were in danger of turning blue when the water temperature fell to almost freezing. The turtles were rescued and taken by truck to a heated swimming pool in a nearby park until the weather warmed up!

*   *   *

One cold February day two mountaineers in Scotland were able to take on an unusual challenge – they climbed a frozen waterfall. It was the Grey Mare's Tail in Dumfries and Galloway and it's sixty metres tall. It took the couple two and a half hours to climb the waterfall's massive icicles even though the fantastic shapes the ice had formed provided natural handholds. But as far as *Newsround* knows it was only done once, for the Grey Mare's Tail was soon its normal rushing watery self again.

*　　　*　　　*

The same winter produced another record from the north of Scotland. On 21 March when spring was well on the way a sheep which had been buried in snow drifts for fifty days was found alive. It had survived on melted snow water; even more incredible it was in excellent condition. Perhaps sheep aren't so silly after all!

*　　　*　　　*

And a combination of animals and freezing weather brought an unexpected problem to the White House in Washington, home of the President of the United States. It was invaded – by mice. An army of them took up residence, and some even got into the Oval office, where the President has his desk. Officials say it could have been embarrassing if they popped up while he was having vital metings. But at least his secrets would have been safe – they'd have been as quiet as mice.

And if it's not weather, it's often weather forecasting which gets a place in *Newsround*. People sometimes believe they can beat the experts, but in Texas a pig farmer made the American weather forecasters feel rather sheepish. The farmer said the weathermen never got the forecast right in his part of Texas. So he challenged them to a contest and the weathermen accepted. The farmer based his forecasts on how his pigs behaved. And, in the experiment, he correctly predicted rainstorms over his farm eight times out of ten. The weathermen, with all their scientific equipment, got it right only once. They insisted they really were good at getting the weather correct over a wide area – but that it was more difficult to say exactly what would happen over Farmer John's fields. Obviously the pigs don't find it too difficult . . .

*　　　*　　　*

Not all amateurs are so successful though. From Australia came the story of John Nash. He predicted that the city of Adelaide would be destroyed by an earthquake and tidal wave. So he moved to a town called Warwick, which he said was the safest place in Australia. Well, nothing happened to Adelaide, but a month after he moved to his new home at Warwick the town had its worst floods for fifty years!

*　　　*　　　*

Happy Landings

Into London's Heathrow Airport one day came a high-flying cat who stowed away on board several airliners and managed to fly half-way round the world. The cat lived on the Pacific island of Guam – they could tell that from his collar – but somehow he'd managed to reach London. Airport officials could not work out how he made the thirteen-thousand mile trip. But they did know that he managed to change planes, un-noticed, in Washington, the American capital. Later the cat who'd joined the jet set was put back on a plane to America, with the status of VIP – Very Important Puss.

*   *   *

The wonder pigeon who flew into the headlines when he arrived back in London first-class aboard a jumbo jet, may have taken everyone for a ride. The pigeon arrived at Heathrow aboard a flight from Canada. Everyone thought that he'd used his own wings to get to Canada after taking a wrong turn on a trip to Manchester. But the crew of the Royal yacht *Britannia* then said that a pigeon fitting his description joined them when they were sailing across to Canada for the tour by the Prince and Princess of Wales. It seems the pigeon travelled in royal style, with a first-class ticket both ways. *Coo*, as the pigeon might say!

*   *   *

Twenty flamingoes were among the VIP's who came in for some special treatment at Heathrow Airport. They spent two whole days with their legs in buckets of hot water after they'd arrived from Uruguay in South America with cramp in their legs. The staff at the quarantine centre immediately hit on the hot-water treatment to cure it. After lots of warm water and massage, the birds were much better and ready to complete their journey to Japan. For that journey though, something even more extraordinary happened to them. They were all put into ladies' stockings to stop them moving and hurting themselves during the flight!

* * *

A giant DC–8 airliner took off from London for Canada one day with some VIP's on board – in this case, VIP stands for Very Important Puppies. In fact, the plane had been specially chartered to fly two puppies across the Atlantic, at a cost of many thousands of pounds. The puppies' owner had been told that if she'd travelled as an ordinary passenger, her puppies would have to go in a crate in the cargo hold. On their *special* flight, the puppies had the front rows of the airliner all to themselves – and the attention of four stewardesses.

* * *

The World of Work

From America came a plan to make children *work* for their television. They would have to generate the electricity themselves if they wanted to view what Americans call 'junk' television – things like cartoons and quizzes. An indoor exercise bike was specially adapted to act as a generator, and the power was stored in a car battery. The system was invented by a doctor in California. Orders for the pedal-telly came in from all over America, even though the doctor's children weren't too keen on the idea themselves. They were allowed to watch information programmes without working for them – I wonder if they would have had to pedal to watch *Newsround*?

*　　*　　*

Also from America came the story of the person who'd been leading a Boy Scout troop for four years but couldn't be called a Scoutmaster – because she's a woman! Mrs Catherine Pollard, of Connecticut, started running the troop because no man would do it. But the Boy Scouts Association of the USA ruled that the twenty-six boys of the troop must have a man to teach them to tie knots and light fires. So Mrs Pollard took the Association to court in an attempt to be officially called a Scoutmaster! It couldn't happen here – the Scouting Association in Britain says that there are already many lady leaders and always have been.

Sending children to work has been against the laws of Great Britain for many years. But in West Germany a judge warned that children who didn't do their fair share of work around the house were breaking the law. He came across an ancient German rule which says children are duty-bound to help their parents. Children under the age of six aren't included – they can just play. But between six and ten, they should help now and again with washing-up and shopping. From ten to fourteen, they should mow the lawn, wash-up, and clean shoes – including their parents' shoes! And from fourteen to sixteen, they should carry out chores like cleaning the car, and heavier work around the house. Pretty clever – those ancient lawyers who'd heard about lawn mowers and motor cars!

*　　　*　　　*

The last of these work stories, like the first, also comes from West Germany. In Mannheim, they found a rather unusual way of tracking down smells caused by pollution. They persuaded eighty-five people with sensitive noses to go round the town, several times a day, *sniffing*. They had to report the worst cases, and a list of these was drawn up in the hope that the city would be a much sweeter place in the future. Whether it worked or not – who nose?

*　　　*　　　*

Classroom Capers

Donald Duck is bad for children. That was the decision of teachers in the Australian state of Queensland, who banned all Donald Duck books and comics. Besides Donald, such famous characters as Pluto, Goofy and even Mickey Mouse, the best-known Disney favourite of all time, will not be seen in Queensland again. The reason the teachers gave was that these well-known cartoon stars stop children inventing characters of their own. Teachers in Britain expressed surprise. They believe that Disney characters are good because they make children read more. Just goes to show, Australians won't stop taking the Mickey.

*   *   *

In Scotland pupils studying for the equivalent of 'O' level will, if they want, be able to be examined on the music of the bagpipe. Bagpipes, except in rare circumstances, can't be played in an orchestra. But now they will be rated along with the piano and the violin. When he heard the news, the Principal of the College of Piping said: 'It's the biggest single encouragement for piping in our lifetime.' And perhaps Jimmy Pryde, who made the top-selling record of 'Amazing Grace' on the bagpipes, had something to do with the change of heart.

*   *   *

School children in Northamptonshire discovered a different kind of painting lesson. The council there encouraged them, together with teachers, to *decorate* their own classrooms – as a way of saving money. All the materials were provided; there was a bonus as well. Fifty pounds extra to spend on books was given to those schools who took up the offer. Maybe if they combined it with maths and did painting by numbers they'd get another award!

*　　*　　*

One story from 1981 was about what must be the most expensive piece of homework in history. Just before Jimmy Carter stopped being the President of the United States, his daughter Amy was asked by her teacher to answer questions about the Industrial Revolution for her weekend homework. She asked her mother for some help. But Mrs Carter couldn't give her any information, so she got in touch with someone at the American Government's Department of Labour. There the message got mixed up, and officials thought it was an urgent request from the President himself. And all sorts of highly-paid civil servants spent the weekend gathering information to put into official reports – all for Amy's history homework.

*　　*　　*

Christmas Crackers

A Christmas story from the USA created a bit of a stink one year. A big park in the state of New Jersey was visited by thieves who stole the Christmas trees. So the park staff sprayed the remaining trees with a chemical that gave off a dreadful smell – it's been described as something between a rotten egg and a skunk. The chemical also stops wild deer in the park from spoiling the trees – but humans don't notice the smell till they get the trees into their homes. And one scent you don't want along with the roasting turkey is the smell of skunk!

*   *   *

Santa doesn't ride through the snow all over the world. In Australia, Christmas comes in the middle of summer, and the temperature on the beaches hovers around the low thirties centigrade – about ninety degrees fahrenheit. So at the Marouba Beach Life-saving Club in Sydney, Santa came in through the surf – and he had a few tips on swimming in safety. After sweltering on the beach in his full regalia, Santa headed back once again to the sea.

*   *   *

More Record Breakers

Is this the deadliest world record ever? In South Africa, a man sat in a room with twenty-four highly poisonous snakes – and stayed there with them for forty days. After he'd been in the room for seventeen days he very nearly gave up. The deadliest of all his snakes, a Black Mamba, was suddenly disturbed. It stuck its fangs into his pillow as he was relaxing on the bed. He didn't give up – but he must have been rattled.

*   *   *

One of the most dangerous stunts ever must have been the amazing tight rope walk high over the city of Rio de Janeiro in South America. A young American, Steve McPeak walked a huge distance in his bare feet along the tight rope which stretched from Mount Urca to Sugar Loaf mountain – four hundred metres high. The 'rope' was, in fact, one of a number of cables used to take tourists between the two mountains in cable-cars. Half-way across, Steve reached the two flags of the United States and Brazil, where he paused to give a salute to the crowds below. The suspense was terrific!

*   *   *

A third record-breaking story which reached *Newsround* in 1981 didn't need any daring at all on the part of a 'competitor'. An old lady whose home was in the Caucasus Mountains of the Soviet Union celebrated her birthday, and nearly seventy of her elderly friends called to wish her well. The unusual aspect was that the birthday was the lady's one hundred and thirtieth, and every one of her friends was over a hundred years old! Is it the mountain air that makes them all live so long. The local candlemaker must be a rich man.

More Animal Antics

The tables were turned one day in Devon when Percy, a tabby cat was attacked. Percy became very upset when a local mouse calmly walked over to his saucer of milk – and started to drink it. Percy moved in smartly to deal with the upstart, but before he could do anything, the mouse attacked. The fearless mouse bit him, taking a slice out of his nose. So his mistress decided to put a saucer down for the mouse as well.

*　　*　　*

A pensioner whose home was near York couldn't understand what was the matter with his new telly. The remote control box kept changing channels, all by itself. The repair men couldn't find anything wrong with the set – but eventually, they tracked down the cause of the trouble. It was Joey, his pet budgie. His cheeping was on the same frequency as the ultra-sonic channel changer. So, when Joey cheeped, the telly changed. Eventually the set was adjusted, so that it couldn't tune in to Joey.

*　　*　　*

Badgers usually avoid human company – they are rather shy creatures. One badger lost all trace of his shyness one morning and wandered right into the village of St Nicholas near Cardiff. Once there he found himself a remarkable new home . . . behind a toilet in a cottage back yard. The badger – a large sixteen kilogramme male – gave the cottage's owner a bit of a fright, so she called for help. Meanwhile, the badger was settled in comfortably. He even went to sleep, and it took an RSPCA inspector over half an hour to coax him into a cage.

*   *   *

Some children in Wiltshire had a couple of unexpected guests at dinner-time one day in April. Their visitors were two lions. It seems they'd escaped from a circus in a neighbouring field. One of them got into Devizes Comprehensive school through a classroom – luckily it was empty at the time. The other jumped through a plate glass window and the noise brought the teachers running. Within minutes, the circus staff were on the scene, and the lions were on their way back home.

*   *   *

On and Off the Tracks

All over the world, railway systems are always in the news. In Japan, the inscrutable faces of the country's railway bosses had a rather embarrassed look about them in the late 1970s. It was because their famous express trains, known as 'Bullets', were brought to a standstill – by some humble crows. They had innocently built their nests in electric pylons beside the tracks, and had caused short circuits, cutting off the power supply to the world's fastest trains. Normally, the 'Bullets' travel at two hundred and ten kilometres an hour, and to stop this kind of thing happening again, the railway officials ordered that the pylons be treated with a bird repellent. Now once again the Bullet trains are something they can crow about.

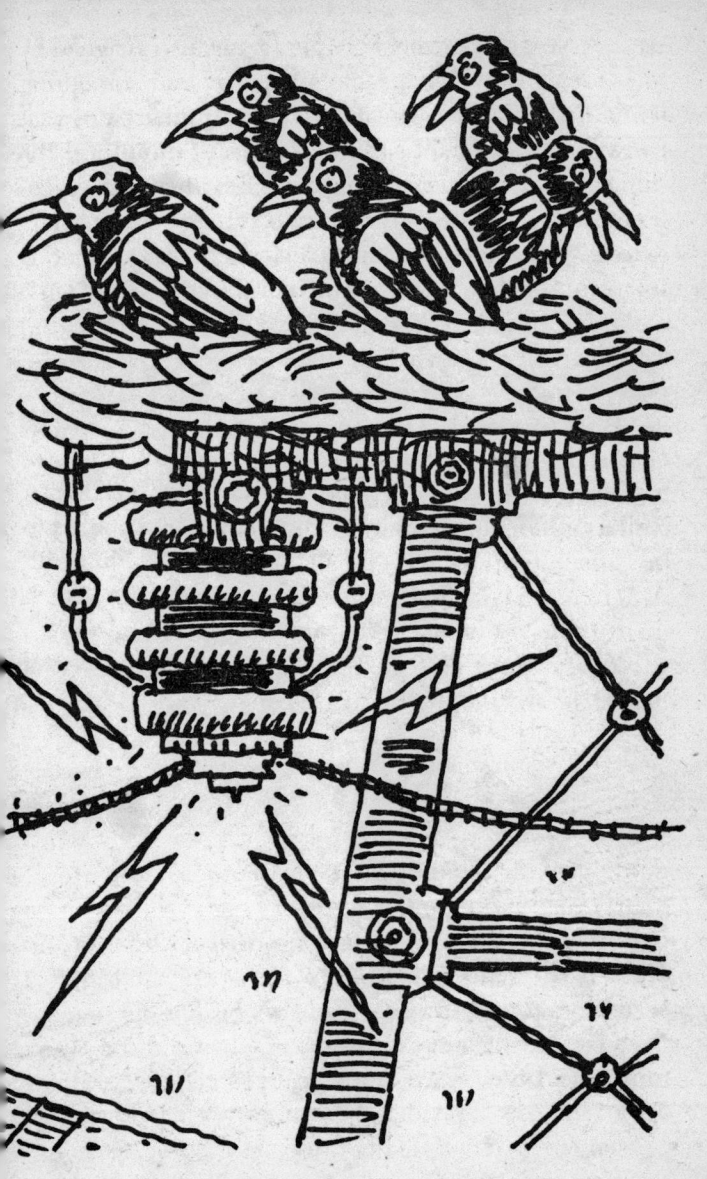

And in New York, where people are always intrigued by new ideas, party-givers have been offered something just a little bit different. They can rent their city's vast railway station, called Grand Central Station, for the night. All it costs is sixty pence! But there's a catch! They also have to pay a 'small' charge for security guards, maintenance men and cleaners. And *that* adds up to another four thousand pounds. Doesn't sound *fare*!

*　　　*　　　*

It was Americans, too, who wanted to buy Victoria Station in London. An American company sent British Rail a bid for this famous landmark. And it claimed to be absolutely serious about the offer − after all, Americans have already bought two other great British institutions: London Bridge, and the luxury cruise ship, the *Queen Mary*. But this time it seems they're out of luck. Victoria definitely isn't for sale.

*　　　*　　　*

And speaking of stations, the station master at Hayes near London got so fed up with people scribbling all over waiting-room walls that he tried an experiment. He put up blank posters, provided pens, and invited scribblers to use them instead. It's been a big success, because hardly anyone scribbles on walls there any more. And now, station masters at five other stations are trying the same idea. Let's hope it's a good way for passengers to let off steam.

Incredible Journeys

Scientists have recently come up with a new theory on how we find our way around. Experts at Manchester University sniffed out the answer by examining human skulls. They discovered that some of the bones in the nose are magnetic. These bones pick up the earth's magnetic field and work just like a compass. This could explain how primitive tribes can find their way across trackless deserts. Modern man doesn't make much use of this skill, although other creatures, such as dolphins, find their way hundreds of kilometres across the oceans. And homing pigeons getting back to their lofts have similar magnetic bones and use them all the time. So next time you're lost when out for a walk you know what to do: just follow your nose!

Whether Silky the Australian tom cat used his nose or not, he certainly made an epic journey. His owner Ken took Silky with him when he went to stay in his caravan at a small place called Gin Gin. He let Silky out for the night, and Silky didn't come back. Well, not for several months. After an incredible journey that covered the huge distance for a cat of two thousand kilometres, Silky arrived home in Melbourne. Ken says his loyal cat was very much the worse for wear after his experience and his paws were a bit rough. But Silky the cat just wouldn't be licked!

*　　　*　　　*

A runaway chimpanzee caused a traffic jam and then jumped into a police car while the officers were trying to sort out the chaos! The chimp, called Joe, escaped from a wildlife park in Warwickshire, and wandered on to a nearby road. First he jumped on to the back of a motorbike, and then, while police were warning drivers to wind up their windows, he nipped into *their* car. Joe accepted a drink with drugs in it, but it didn't knock him out. Instead, he jumped into a tree and stayed there until he was finally recaptured, after three hours of freedom. Police said no one was hurt in the escapade, but at times, it was a bit hairy!

*　　　*　　　*

In 1981 a visitor stranded on a beach in Lincolnshire was more than sixteen hundred kilometres off course. She was a two-year old walrus – only the fourth to be found along Britain's coastline so far this century. Walrus rarely travel south of the Arctic Ocean. This one was so heavy that local naturalists turned a tarpaulin sheet into a chute to launch her back into the sea. What a send off!

*   *   *

Another Arctic story was about a pregnant polar bear that got scientists from the two super powers, America and the Soviet Union, working together. The previous summer, American scientists had fitted the bear with a tiny radio transmitter. This emitted a series of 'bleeps' which enabled her journey to be plotted by use of a satellite tuned in to the transmitter. The Americans plotted her journey from Alaska to the Arctic. Then it seemed she strayed across the ice floes into Russia where the Americans couldn't follow. But there's good co-operation in the scientific field, and Russian scientists took on the task of following her. In April, when she had been plodding for eight hundred kilometres through snow, the bear stopped. The scientists had to assume she'd made a den and had a baby. Later they tracked her on her homeward trip, and 'handed her back' to the Americans.

*   *   *

Another incredible journey was made by a British cat called Lucky. One April she wandered into a warehouse and got trapped in a packing case bound for America. So Lucky crossed the Atlantic by cargo boat, surviving for seven weeks without food or drink. At the beginning of September she was flown home – a Lucky cat in more than just name.

*   *   *

Another stowaway was a three-year-old tabby cat called William. He overcame the bad winter weather and train strikes of 1979 to travel several hundred kilometres by British Rail ... for nothing. William disappeared a week before Christmas from his home which backs on to railway sidings in Lancaster, then turned up over three hundred kilometres away in Newport. William, the inter-city kitty.

*   *   *

The local council on the Isle of Skye decided to make life easier for the island's population of hedgehogs. The roads department was worried about the plight of unwary hedgehogs who fall through cattle grids while crossing the road. So it decided to put ramps inside the grids so the creatures could clamber out. But the hedgehogs will still have to watch out for the road hogs.

Problem Pets

Lots of stories which reach *Newsround* are about wild animals or pets, and usually they have a happy ending. One such came from Iran in the Middle East. It's all about a white donkey that belonged to a man called Musht Jaafar. One day it was stolen and eventually Musht gave up hope of ever finding it again. So he went to the market in the town of Sahr-E-Kord and bought a new donkey, a black one. On the way home it started to rain . . . and slowly, the black donkey began to turn white. And Mr Jaafar turned red. He realised he'd bought his own donkey, which the thieves had dyed black . . . until the rain started to wash it out!

Then there was Winston the labrador from Bradford-on-Avon, near Bath. For many years he had waited at a crossroads, looking for his lost owner who never turned up. And Winston was 'adopted' by people at a nearby hospital. But then came plans to move the hospital to another building in a different part of town, and local people were asked to vote on whether they wanted this to happen. And the question of what would happen to Winston really worried the voters. He had become a two-kennel dog – one by the crossroads, and one that was built for him in the hospital grounds. He was getting old and set in his ways, and people were concerned whether he would survive if all his friends at the hospital moved away. Many of them said they'd only vote for the move if Winston went as well. Then the hospital's League of Friends came to the rescue. They agreed to pay the cost of moving Winston and his kennels to the new site.

*   *   *

Millie was an overweight budgie, who had just a bit too much bounce. Poor Millie grew so fat from eating too much of her favourite food, millet, that she could hardly get off the ground. And when she actually did try to fly she dropped like a stone. So the vet put Millie on a strict diet. Within weeks the unwanted flab melted away. The budgie that couldn't budge took to the air. And Millie was once more light as a feather.

Another stranded animal drew the attention of fishermen and the Royal Navy. A killer whale, quickly nicknamed Dopey Dick, swam inland from the North Atlantic for about forty kilometres and was seen not far from Londonderry in Northern Ireland. Dopey Dick swam right through some underwater nets set by the army across the river mouth and happily enjoyed a diet of best Londonderry salmon. After several days in the river, Royal Navy boats tried to make Dopey swim back to sea. It wasn't because he was unpopular – there were traffic jams galore with Dopey's fans watching from a bridge – but everyone was worried he wouldn't survive in the shallow river water. Then local fishermen tried, but they were no more successful than the Navy. After five days, one morning Dopey was no longer to be seen. He must have swum out to sea again – presumably after having a whale of a time.

An equally amazing story was about a goldfish – thought to be dead – that survived two days at the bottom of a rubbish bin. Its owner found the little fish floating, apparently dead, in his pond. He threw it in the bin with the rubbish. Two days later, when he saw its tail wriggle, he realised it was still alive. He put it in some warm water and soon it was swimming around merrily again. What a fishy tale!

Lucky Dip

The exotic eastern art of belly dancing was studied by a group of mums in Hertfordshire – as a way of keeping themselves slim. The village school at Watton was the unlikely setting for the course in belly dancing. But the teacher claimed that the exercises really would knock off kilos in weight in just a few weeks – and be much more fun than ordinary keep-fit classes. The six house-wives made their costumes themselves, and said they'd entertain their families and friends with their dancing.

*   *   *

A hair-raising story reached *Newsround* one day from Australia. A new cure for baldness could be on the way thanks to an ancient gypsy remedy. The idea came from a lady who lives in Queensland. As a child she'd been told by a gypsy healer of a powerful lotion containing thirteen different herbs which could prevent hair falling out. Well, Ma, as she's known, made the secret lotion for some balding friends at her local bingo club. And it worked so well that a wealthy businessman paid her seven hundred thousand pounds for the recipe! Eventually it'll be available worldwide. Hope it's not a case of hair today, gone tomorrow!

*   *   *

The splendours of Brighton, one of Britain's most famous seaside towns, gained a new attraction in 1980. The town opened a beach for naturists – people who like to swim and sunbathe without any clothes on. There was a huge row over whether it should be allowed in the middle of town, in clear view of everyone on the promenade. Only a couple of people turned up the first morning because it was very cold for swimming. Many would-be swimmers may have noticed the dateline of April 1 and decided only a fool would have a try.

You might also enjoy reading these other BBC/Knight titles:

PUZZLE TRAIL

CLIVE DOIG

Based on BBC television's immensely popular *Puzzle Trail*, this book is guaranteed to provide hours of fun, frustration and entertainment.

THE SECOND BOOK OF JIGSAW PUZZLES
THE THIRD BOOK OF JIGSAW PUZZLES
JIGSAW PUZZLES 4

CLIVE DOIG

Three entertaining books filled with puzzles and word games, based on BBC television's award-winning *Jigsaw* programme.

RENTAGHOST ENTERPRISES

BOB BLOCK

Fans of the hilarious *Rentaghost* television series are sure
to enjoy reading about their favourite spooks.